My Journey through Grief

Copyright Jen Carter 2018

I'm so sorry that you're here.

There are no words that will bring you comfort right now. I've been through deep loss and tragedy myself, so I'm speaking from personal experience.

This grief journal includes some prompts, or sentence completion ideas. Feel free to use them, or ignore them. This journal is for you to use (or not use), just as you choose.

Feel free to splurge all those feelings and words that you don't dare to share with anyone else right now. It's OK for your emotion to fill the pages of this journal.

There is no right way to use this journal. Do whatever works for you.

With love,
Jennifer

_____

I feel sad today because:

I'd like to tell you:

I felt calmer today when:

You taught me:

_____

I feel alone today because:

I feel more stressed when:

I feel better when:

What I'm remembering about you today:

_____

I got upset today because:

Things are different now because:

I feel accepted when:

What I miss most is:

_____

| I worry about: |

| I want you to know: |

| Since you've been gone: |

| I wish you: |

_____

I feel sad today because:

I'd like to tell you:

I felt calmer today when:

You taught me:

_____

I feel alone today because:

I feel more stressed when:

I feel better when:

What I'm remembering about you today:

_____

I got upset today because:

Things are different now because:

I feel accepted when:

What I miss most is:

_____

I worry about:

I want you to know:

Since you've been gone:

I wish you:

_____

I feel sad today because:

I'd like to tell you:

I felt calmer today when:

You taught me:

_____

| I feel alone today because: |

| I feel more stressed when: |

| I feel better when: |

| What I'm remembering about you today: |

_____

I got upset today because:

Things are different now because:

I feel accepted when:

What I miss most is:

_____

I worry about:

I want you to know:

Since you've been gone:

I wish you:

_____

I feel sad today because:

I'd like to tell you:

I felt calmer today when:

You taught me:

_____

I feel alone today because:

I feel more stressed when:

I feel better when:

What I'm remembering about you today:

_____

| I got upset today because: |

| Things are different now because: |

| I feel accepted when: |

| What I miss most is: |

_____

I worry about:

I want you to know:

Since you've been gone:

I wish you:

_____

I feel sad today because:

I'd like to tell you:

I felt calmer today when:

You taught me:

_____

I feel alone today because:

I feel more stressed when:

I feel better when:

What I'm remembering about you today:

_____

I got upset today because:

Things are different now because:

I feel accepted when:

What I miss most is:

_____

I worry about:

I want you to know:

Since you've been gone:

I wish you:

_____

I feel sad today because:

I'd like to tell you:

I felt calmer today when:

You taught me:

_____

I feel alone today because:

I feel more stressed when:

I feel better when:

What I'm remembering about you today:

_____

I got upset today because:

Things are different now because:

I feel accepted when:

What I miss most is:

_____

| I worry about: |

| I want you to know: |

| Since you've been gone: |

| I wish you: |

_____

I feel sad today because:

I'd like to tell you:

I felt calmer today when:

You taught me:

_____

| I feel alone today because: |

| I feel more stressed when: |

| I feel better when: |

| What I'm remembering about you today: |

_____

I got upset today because:

Things are different now because:

I feel accepted when:

What I miss most is:

_____

I worry about:

I want you to know:

Since you've been gone:

I wish you:

_____

I feel sad today because:

I'd like to tell you:

I felt calmer today when:

You taught me:

_____

I feel alone today because:

I feel more stressed when:

I feel better when:

What I'm remembering about you today:

_____

I got upset today because:

Things are different now because:

I feel accepted when:

What I miss most is:

_____

I worry about:

I want you to know:

Since you've been gone:

I wish you:

_____

I feel sad today because:

I'd like to tell you:

I felt calmer today when:

You taught me:

_____

I feel alone today because:

I feel more stressed when:

I feel better when:

What I'm remembering about you today:

_____

| I got upset today because: |

| Things are different now because: |

| I feel accepted when: |

| What I miss most is: |

_____

I worry about:

I want you to know:

Since you've been gone:

I wish you:

_____

I feel sad today because:

I'd like to tell you:

I felt calmer today when:

You taught me:

_____

I feel alone today because:

I feel more stressed when:

I feel better when:

What I'm remembering about you today:

_____

I got upset today because:

Things are different now because:

I feel accepted when:

What I miss most is:

_____

I worry about:

I want you to know:

Since you've been gone:

I wish you:

_____

I feel sad today because:

I'd like to tell you:

I felt calmer today when:

You taught me:

_____

I feel alone today because:

I feel more stressed when:

I feel better when:

What I'm remembering about you today:

_____

| I got upset today because: |

| Things are different now because: |

| I feel accepted when: |

| What I miss most is: |

_____

I worry about:

I want you to know:

Since you've been gone:

I wish you:

_____

I feel sad today because:

I'd like to tell you:

I felt calmer today when:

You taught me:

_____

| I feel alone today because: |

| I feel more stressed when: |

| I feel better when: |

| What I'm remembering about you today: |

_____

I got upset today because:

Things are different now because:

I feel accepted when:

What I miss most is:

_____

I worry about:

I want you to know:

Since you've been gone:

I wish you:

Other books by Jennifer Carter:

Daily Readings for Difficult Days - a daily devotional for Christian women going through difficult times, including divorce, death of a loved one, depression, and other struggles. Find inspiration and encouragement as Jennifer shares stories, bible readings and personal testimony.

Women of Courage - explores the lives of inspiring women from the Bible, through thirty-one daily bible readings. In a quest to understand what a Godly woman looks like, Jennifer examines the often untold stories of thirty-one women in the Bible.

Each of these remarkable women has much to teach us. They led busy lives and experienced challenges, disappointments and triumphs. Yet each found fruitfulness, purpose and contentment.

Their stories can inspire us to be more courageous and help us find our place in God's plans and purposes.

Available on Kindle, Audible and as a paperback book.

www.ingramcontent.com/pod-product-compliance
Lightning Source LLC
Chambersburg PA
CBHW081338080526
44588CB00017B/2659